Bitterroot

New Women's Voices Series, No. 143

poems by

Jessica Jones

Finishing Line Press
Georgetown, Kentucky

Bitterroot

For Emily, Isaiah, Eugene,
and all my other Montana kiddos

ACKNOWLEDGMENTS

Many thanks to those presses who gave a few of these poems first homes under slightly
different guises:

".22" originally appeared in *Poems across the Big Sky*, (Many Voices Press, 2016)
"Ghosts" and "New Girl" are included in *Bright Bones* (Open Country Press, 2018).

As a collection, *Bitterroot* was a runner-up for the Open Country Press Chapbook
Competition (2017), and a semi-finalist with *Cutbank* at the University of Montana (2018).

Sincere thanks to Finishing Line Press for choosing to put this collection in print, to
Christen Kincaid for handling the final details, and to Kent State University at Stark for
travel funding to numerous conferences and readings.

I am also indebted to many learning communities: The University of Montana and Payne
Native American Center, the "Worlds Apart But Not Strangers" TOLI Institute, the Montana
Indian Education Association, Salish Kootenai College, the Missoula Writing Collaborative,
and my wonderful teacher friends across Montana.

Deepest gratitude to the individuals who helped these poems find form: Robert Lee
& Rosemary Lynch for the coffee sessions in Missoula, Twila Old Coyote and Alyssa
Arrowtop for the opportunity to write and read amidst Upward Bound folks, my mother
for the occasional perfect word (and for knowing my heart when my pen did not). Much
appreciation to Naatosi Fish for cultural and linguistic guidance and a deep bow to my
mentor, David Moore for the generous knowledge and keen musical ear.

I am blessed to be a part of such a rich and ever-widening circle.

Publisher: Leah Maines
Editor: Christen Kincaid
Cover Art: Jessica Jones
Author Photo: Roxene Dialesandro
Cover Design: Leah Huete

Printed in the USA on acid-free paper.
Order online: www.finishinglinepress.com
            also available on amazon.com

Author inquiries and mail orders:
Finishing Line Press
P. O. Box 1626
Georgetown, Kentucky 40324
U. S. A.

Table of Contents

Set in montana

Preface

This collection draws from several years of teaching public school in Western Montana, primarily on the Flathead Indian Reservation, where I also lived and mentored at a local youth home.

The Flathead is a "checkerboard rez," meaning that land which was once wholly inhabited by Indigenous peoples has been repeatedly broken up, given to Whites and reduced, leading to complicated intersections of Native and non-Native cultures, ownership and co-habitation.

Despite the purposeful erasure of Native oppression from most U.S. history books, in recent years Montana has fought hard for formal Indian Education training for all teachers. Currently, 30% of Montana public school curriculum must attend to addressing formerly marginalized knowledge, now organized and accessible via the Montana Office of Public Instruction.

With this highly charged, multifaceted history in mind, I respectfully admit that I will never fully know this land or its inhabitants. I write as an ally: a teacher and youth advocate humbled by both the complexity of Montana's Indian Country and by the celebration of its cultural "survivance," to use a term from Anishinaabe scholar Gerald Vizenor. I remain grateful to all those who continue to teach me.

The names and revealing details of students, teachers and community members in this collection have been changed and omitted. Other names, such as friends, willing colleagues, public figures and local establishments remain unaltered.

—PART I—

St. Mary's Mission

Sleeping in the shadow of St. Mary's Peak,
ghosts of the Bitterroot Salish.
White ladies
smile as they watch I don't steal
rosaries or Mexican crèches,
postcards with the story of
"Stevensville—Where Montana began."
Another story moans softly
on a breeze behind the church.
A cross for Indians outside the cemetery
may as well read, "Savages here."

The third Sunday of September
the tribe is "welcome" to visit
their homeland,
sing Father Ravalli's hymns in Salish.
"He brought small pox vaccines," a church lady
tells me. "*They* brought blankets
and bear skins and sat on the floor."
Minerals from the Judith River
paint the altar yellow.
"They fought that," she confesses.
"Yellow means *victory* to the Salish."

I study the photo
of a Salish woman and her baby,
"Visit Home, 1911"
twenty years after a government-forced
march eighty miles north
to the Reservation.
Her eyes are warm,
perhaps with the stories
she knows will fill her belly
when winter is cold
in the Jocko.

Saturday Night Bluegrass at the Methodist Church

That Moiese cowboy with fire green eyes
broke all kind of dams in me.
His baritone twang and how
he regarded his wife and son
when he returned to their table.

I sat with an old couple;
didn't go up
but could have—
    Take me Home and Hold Watcha Got… and
    … Daddy won't you take me back

    To Muhlenberg County
    Down by the Green River
    Where Paradise lay…
        familiar bronze chords
        Ohio's long sweetness still in my veins.

A lady in a red dress
with her hair dyed too black
took the mic and tried her best notes;
the banjo player
still nodded politely.

When I left they called, "Come back,
come back! And bring your fiddle!"
    (My violin asleep
    Coty's Wild Musk and vanilla
    still breathing in its rosewood curve,

        2000 miles away—)
But tonight was enough.
The wide Mission Valley lit
with dusky clouds
my drive north.

[handwritten annotation:] about her time in a Church singing Bluegrass music with the town people

[handwritten annotation:] It goes out to the person who helped her eldit the book

5

Pablo Transfer Station

Sunday afternoon
I climbed the mound
of Bee Mill kindling
in dusty gloves
and baseball hat,
squinting under the sun.

A woman with a flatbed
asked if I knew her sister;
I didn't, but it felt nice to be asked.
Took a photo of the wood heap
to send home:
Only in Montana...

Stopped by the IGA for an iced tea;
brown-eyed children
playing hide and seek
in the freezer aisle
their grandfather catching up
with the clerk.

Drove south, windows down
my backseat and trunk loaded with pine
saw Jezebel McCaffrey
skipping along 93
near the trailer park
little sister in tow, laughing.

Jez who
rarely attends 6th grade
for migraines or strep
or lack of a ride
(last Wednesday
in all black, with cat ears)

this warm September day,
white legs kicking
red hair aglow—
pied beauty
face tilted toward the sun.

Field Trip

The 6th grade tried to fish
Kicking Horse.
While grownups assembled rods,
doled out line, hooked worms,
kids were each to cast twice.
But Will dropped his meds in the gravel,
Cheyenna lost her glasses,
everyone wanted sunscreen.
Jazlyn slipped in the mud,
the outhouse was a hike....
When the busses rolled in too soon,
Mr. Valor got so mad
students were scared to board.

Returned to the shade
of my classroom,
with chairs stacked
and twenty minutes to kill,
we hung our trout mobiles
from the ceiling then played
a game of metaphors.
Just as the bell rang, Elijah shouted,
"Miss Jones… has more curves
than a racetrack!"
and darted,
leaving me in sudden quiet
under a school of paper fish,

their colored fins gently swimming
in and out
so very soundless.

Boarding Schools

At the Indian Ed Conference, Crow Agency,
the gallery is lined with photos.

Sioux, Cheyenne, Pawnee children
        as young as five years old forced to leave their families
        not given back until eighteen
        taught "American" skills,
        industrial arts
        useless on the Plains.

Inuit children hauled to Pennsylvania,
Navajo, Little Shell, Blackfeet
            forced to strip their clothes,
            erase their names,
            learn the same foreign tongue.

I can't stop staring at one photo,
        "Boys and Girls in Back of Mission Truck, 1928.
        Children coming from Cut Bank Boarding School."
            Twenty-four kids, crowded in coats, hats
            —their faces
            achingly familiar—could be
            Noah, Eneasa, Kamiah, Kree…
            big eyes, soft cheeks,
            the same dimpled fingers
            that trace the desks in my room
            each morning.

It was not until 1978, the presenter's voice floats between didactics, *that Native American parents gained the right to deny their children's placement in off-reservation schools.*

        A man behind me is telling a woman
        they cut off his braids
        beat his knuckles;
        how he carried a sliver of soap in his pocket,
        forced to eat it when he slipped into Crow.
        That everyone, even his friends, said,

                don't speak, don't speak, don't speak.

Woodstove

About her father

When Dad came out to Montana
to visit my Ronan farmhouse,
his first priority was heat.
We donned flannels and gloves
and emptied the ash box
for the two-log burner in my kitchen;
He taught me how to bed it,
damper it down, open the flu
with familiar
patience.

How she was able to bond together

I woke the first morning to an orange glow
flickering beneath my door,
coffee gurgling,
Dad tinkering in slippered feet.
Could hear the swing of stove hinge
iron poker pushing coals,
and I lay like a child, holding on
to each molecule of light and sound:
my father in the content simplicity
of being.

Each day we crossed items off his list:
Outlet switch, hornet's nest, kindling.
And each morning before light rose
over the mountains
we pulled chairs to the window,
watched pink streak the sky
waited for the deer and her twins
to totter from shadows and feed
in frosted yard. We spoke in hushed voices,
sipped coffee.

For three days after he left
our chairs sat facing the prairie.

New Girl

The secretary brings a new girl
to my door during class—
Azda, from New Mexico,
with round cheeks and brown skin.
She buries her face in her mother's breast;
Ms. Azee' measures me with one glass eye,
stroking her daughter's hair.

Azda blurts out in class and steals
like a three-year-old.
During one lunch detention
tells me how her parents leave
for weeks at a time
even when it's cold,
just her and the dog.

Early November, she's absent three days
then shows up at lunch and whispers,
  "I had LICE."
In December, her folks get a stove
for their trailer;
she misses school to get wood but bounces
in her boots in homeroom, "It's WARM!"

One grammar lesson
I catch her with an illustrated book
of Navajo poems, entirely focused.
During spelling she begs colored pencils,
draws Karana, from *Island of the Blue Dolphins*[1]
in full regalia beside her dog,
abandoned by the Aleuts.

---

[1]Island of the Blue Dolphins is a young adult novel loosely (and controversially) based on the true story of an Indigenous woman abandoned on San Nicolas Island as the result of colonialism. Left to survive with only her dog as companion, she is "rescued" eighteen years later by missionaries only to learn that her tribe perished as the result of forced migration, and no one remains to speak her language.

Ovando Christmas Pageant

I arrive just after dusk at Rose and Robert Lee's
for their annual trek to the one-room schoolhouse
in Ovando.

Robert, who fishes over an ice-hole Sundays
and "the lovely Rose," with auburn hair even in her sixties,
present me a gift:

crimson and black hand-woven cap
which I wear, shivering in the backseat
fifty miles east, along the Blackfoot River.

The schoolhouse is packed:
elves in the bathroom, cowboys with shaved necks,
on folding chairs, strong wives, babies.

(Rose and I turn up as enchanted spectators
next day in the *Missoulian*; my chin
peeking around her shoulder.)

After, we cross black ice—shortchanging stars
(12 below and dropping)
to Trixi's Antler Saloon

toast cherry-pink neons, elk heads
and everyone else who thinks whiskey
is a good idea.

Robert says, "When we part
each morning Rose and I kiss
for a reason—"

goes 40 the whole dark way home,
easing the brakes when a shaggy elk
saunters along our headlight beams.

(A year later he writes of a "strange and horrific
accident on that road"—a college boy killed when
an animal bounced off a lady's fender

About going to a play and on the way home telling a story about a boy being killed. She doesn't remember it that way she remembers stars and ice.

11

and into the boy's front seat.) What I remember
from Ovando, though, is stars. Stars and ice
and the shock of our short inward breath.

Coyote Classroom

When I told my students
our unit would include
Skinkoots tales,
bedlam ensued.
"No, no!" they cried. "You can't—
not until there's snow on the ground
or you'll get snakes in your bed."

It's true,
what they said.
So I read, on my own,
Frank B. Linderman's
Kootenai Why Stories
about Co-pee the Owl, Frog Chief
and other Animal People
until it was time.

At which point it grew clear:
Every damn kid in my room
was a trickster.

Hauling Wood

I've tried, but I can't swing an axe.
So one Saturday in February
Arnold drives me
20 minutes into the mountains
outside St. Ignatius, to his property.
We pass wooly horses at the neighbors
and stop to borrow a truck with new chains
then locate two recently fallen trees.

Arnold is wearing a neon long-sleeve shirt
that says "world's toughest volunteers,"
and as he works, yellow wood chips
dust the snow.
I walk part way up the mountain,
listen to moss swishing from the firs
and recall suddenly that
nature is terrifying.

When I return, he's driven down the Skid-steer
to load logs but the brush is too thick.
Truck tires have chewed up black earth
under two feet of snow
and so we use the sled.
On the way into the woods
I ride—shrieking over bumps and dips;
on the way out, I push, shoes slipping under me.

Hours later, my cords and socks in the dryer,
he hands me his ex-wife's snow pants and Sorrel boots.
"It's okay," he says. "One time I found some other man's
socks on the deck and she played dumb."
When we reach the St. Ignatius Malt Shop
for grilled cheese, I feel small and important
at the same time, clomping around
in those big boots.

Valentine's Dance

Such a flurry—the day of a dance.
Snow is still blue, dark out my window
when they trickle in. *Who's-going*

and what-are-you-wearing
Miss-Jones? That-skirt? I like its roses
(Bridger eyeing my ankles

as I hang his pink paper chain
above our door.)
By noon

my desk overflows:
carnations, cupcakes, caramels in a heart-shaped tin,
lunch apples, even a lemon

from someone's kitchen.
The empty-handed lure cookies
from dark pockets, give me eraser-less pencils.

When the bell rings
we race home;
by seven, return to fill a darkened gym.

Billy Joe paces in black shirt, red tie;
girls float by
in white dresses....

The shy ones huddle, beginning
unfinished sentences
while their eyes dart about.

We teachers are shocked:
a three-dollar ticket and Friday night ride,
too much for most.

But here they are—busting the Disco,
the Windshield Wiper, the Swim,
and some other move I can only call the "Flop"—

In a dark corner
even my quietest boy giving it up
to the arms-flying-head-down-all-out Cross-Country Ski.

Paddling Mission Dam

My oar dips
along paddleboard—
smooth, quiet,
Arnold far across
out of sight.
I watch 18 feet below:
tree stumps, fish
in the reeds near shore,
where a friend recently
saw two grizzlies.

Spring chill, first outing.
I kneel
to slow up,
search bottom.
And, as I glide:
two curved spines
beneath me—
four feet each
skulls and jaws still attached
ribs glowing white.

Fish Tacos at Claire's

The Cheff son
built a low-slung adobe
with rough beams and a long hall
that glows like a Georgia O'Keefe.

One warm evening his wife Claire
invited me and a Bangkok friend
for champagne
her parents sent from France.

While their husbands toyed in the barn
we talked under red dusty sun:
my first year in town; Claire's sweet little girl,
the friend's Thai massage.

During dinner, a cow gave birth.
Marc ran out with a flashlight to check
and came back concerned that her milk
hadn't dropped.

There was ice cream with fresh strawberries
for dessert; the couples laughed about
camping trips
when they were newlywed.

As I left, Claire waved from the back step
where heat rose from the rocks
and envy coiled in me
like a snake

poised to eat
the flower of gratitude.

—PART II—

Driving Lake County

I don't remember where we were going—
June in the Mission Valley,
the wide farms outside St. Ignatius—
in the old Subaru.
I took shotgun, Arnold's little girl in back
cello music trembling from the speakers.

As sun slanted toward dusk
every thistle glowed,
each wheat shaft gained a halo;
irrigation pipes sent
arcs of rose-colored mist
across the acres.

I ached for that drive to last forever,
Arnold's rough hand in mine,
feet propped on the dash
before chipped windshield,
feeling deep in the cavity
of my chest

that these two warm laughing bodies
and distant blue mountains
were all I wanted.

Big Dipper Ice Cream, Missoula

I recognized him from my drive through the Jette
night before—73 miles north, rim of Flathead Lake.
His grubby black sweatpants, bike
saddled with bags, how he pushed
the whole rig, rather than rode.

Arnold and I watched him eye the menu
then walk away. "Hey Bicycle!"
Arnold shouted, "You want something?"
The man shuffled forward:
"A strawberry shake. And a chocolate cone."

He told us about Vietnam, The Holy Spirit and Tests ...
A wall in India that goats could climb straight down.
Said he was killed in the military but God brought him back.
That we forget—we forget—
we used to be invisible.

He asked for another cone
and Arnold bought it,
shaking his head, eyes wet as the man
rolled away—Higgins Bridge,
golden Montana evening.

Afterward we swam in the river
in our clothes.

Outlaws

Once, at a restaurant in Gardiner, Montana
my sister and I
ate an entire pizza. Laughed
so hard we spilled the red zin
and laughed some more.

It started... with listing our top
ten memories, then fifty,
until our waitress and bus boy
smiled shy, suspicious smiles
and other tables turned, amused.

Even the jars of pepper flakes and parmesan
gleamed, happy—
our exclamations and flying gestures
floating up
to beams and antlers.

When asked
which check,
I heard
the bus boy say:
"The Sisters."

As we gathered jackets
and brushed off crumbs,
hotel bound—
this night, too,
became folded like a napkin:

...What was the name of
that place
outside Wyoming—
the one
where you spilled the wine...?

Fire Road Trail, Missoula

Half-way up Sentinel,
full sun, late evening July,
I realize grasshoppers
are blessing my path.
Or laughing—
I can't tell which.
Dozens, with each footfall:
pale yellow, papery,
springing
two feet in the air,
perfect arcs
self-propelled confetti.

I nearly miss
the occasion,
wade on
until a pause: they vanish
a step: they leap
from dust,
scorched tumbleweeds,
the mountain
so parched
it might combust
and I—suddenly awake—
amid incandescent flames.

Marginalia

In 1995, Billings, Montana responded to a series of hate crimes
        by printing menorahs in the local paper for everyone to hang,
        sending paint crews to Native, Black and Jewish homes,
        ruined by swastikas,
        campaigning the message: Not in Our Town.

Twenty years later
        teachers make white cranes of KKK bibles
        transpose diagrams of slaves packed into the belly of a ship,
        whisper
            give them names
            give them all names

                (Is it possible
                to bring back passenger pigeons from extinction?)

Indigenous children don't have Truth and Reconciliation unless they read
between the lines:

                America is singing in its rivers' names
                the voices of disc jockeys
                who flip Navajo and English
                like coins
                on 960 AM, New Mexico.

Ask—We urge from the chalkboard—*keep asking*—

        Whose voice is missing? Who flutters on the margin of the page,
            the schoolyard,
        the city limits waiting—   *to interject?*

About the people with the unheard
Voices. Having to do with teaching
and being able to hear people who
havent been heard

Canal Boys

To come and go from the cabin
there's a wooden bridge above a canal
that comes down from the mountain
glacial cold and coursing fast enough
to rip your shoulder out of socket.

The neighbor, Jim, built it twenty years back
and tells me in his soft, stern voice,
not to mess around. He watched his buddy bleed
out in Vietnam, does not take death

or avoiding it
lightly.

Two boys drowned, he says, six years back

and every time I cross my mind explodes—
        was it curiosity? King-of-the-hill?
        An unfair moment of innocence?
        Perhaps a warning—

        just enough to taste its force
        feel that delicious water
        ride its straight arrow
        three miles to where the spillway
        churns white, perpetual.

The eight-year-old slipped, I finally learn, taking pictures
and his brother dove in
after.

From Oswego[1] —sparse prairie town near Wolf Point,
survived by two sisters, Cherish Rose and Mourning Dove.

When spring comes I imagine them beneath an air hole
in semi-frozen tributary,
eyes opening to clumps of bear grass, black water
        Waiting.

---

[1] "Pouring-out-place," a river's mouth.

.22

It's hunting season on Flathead Rez.
Polson Wal-Mart is full of gaitered men,
in Carhartts; my 6th graders
miss class to fill their tags.
The principal's daughter points
to a loaded Ford, "My Dad got a bear last night!"
and everyone races to the window.

One morning I hold up a dream catcher
from Tribal Days.
"The tassles," I explain,
"are crimped shotgun shells,"
but fifteen voices shout from their seats,
"That's not a shot gun—that's a .22!"
and I am once again the student.

mid October early november

—I liked how you were able to include hunting season in the book and what the town was like—

Power Outage

The power is out tonight for line upgrades
at Seliš Ksanka Qlispe Dam.
From now til morning,
West Shore and Finley Point
to Hot Springs and Camas Prairie,
the Rez is off grid.
The house has settled so deeply
into its bones
I can hear Rupert snoring
softly on the floor below.

If I strain, I might
hear coyote padding
along the shores
of Flathead Lake
an hour north,
his tracks a dotted line.
For miles, no flicker
but the stars and a memory
of nights, which until
this pin-drop
of time stretched
back and back
into the lapping
darkness
of forever
. . . .
. . . .
. . . . .
. . .
.

Winter Festival

*Staff: Winter break is short because
students rely on school breakfast and lunch.
Please be mindful of the poverty in our district.
Some kids get broken promises for Christmas.*

—*Principal's December Memo*

It's dark in Montana this time of year,
light not rising until homeroom
and leaving quickly after the four o'clock bell,
with leaden clouds and black mountains between.

My 6th graders read Lois Red Elk's "Winter Solstice,"
Robert Frost's, "Stopping by Woods,"
quietly reciting: *The-only-other-sound's-the-sweep
Of-easy-wind-and-downy-flake....*

Each day we slowly transform our classroom
with hand-written poems and glitter;
snowflakes and white twinklers
strung across chalk board and shelves....

Until they arrive, Friday,
wide-eyed—lights low, everything glowing,
our cookies ready for delivery
to lunch ladies and staff.

I weave a story about a village girl
who discovers the secret
to this darkest day is sharing
and give them each a "solstice stone,"

small ovals of blue glass.
To my surprise
they receive them open-palmed,
slipping them carefully into pockets and backpacks,

our magic undisturbed
but for one boy, who whispers urgently at the door,
Are solstice stones really real?
I want so badly to say, *Yes.*

North Star

Years after the boarding school era,
"It is estimated that one in every four girls
and one in every seven boys
will be victims of sexual abuse in Indian Country,
according to the Indian Health Service."
—"Kootenai Dance in the New Year,"
Missoulian, January 5, 2006

Janet comes in at lunch
to work on her Harriet Tubman paper.
She can read but barely writes.
Always in long shorts and a dirty flannel,
hair chopped short;
only talks to cousins.

She and Cherith hop by my bookshelves,
arms linked: "Miss Jones, did you know it's bad
if you fall at jump dances?"
When I call on Janet during class
Cherith shakes her head:
"She won't read out loud."

I crouch by her table now, beside the tray
of soggy smiley fries and chicken strips.
"So there was like an underground railroad?" she asks.
"Tunnels," I say, "and secret passage ways."
"Cool," she says. Then,
"This lady was like beat in the head and stuff."

Janet does not know I know
about the sunk-in trailer with blankets for walls,
her dead mother's gun and which uncle
should be in jail. I leave her,
pencil in hand, to navigate
constellations of unimaginable darkness.

Then she's absent two weeks.
When she finds the Tubman notes in her locker
they're punctured with hundreds of pencil holes.
"Janet," I tease,
"Did you make me a lace doily?"
She breaks into a grin and shrugs.

Oh, Janet. Does the north star
still point to freedom?

White Out

Ravalli Hill is a bitch in the snow.
I've got studded tires
and a sturdy little Toyota
and still I'm creeping ten miles an hour
down that curve
past the Bison Range.
Near the exit for 200
I see a few tiny flares
hot pink through the squall
and two road men trudging
between mountain
and a car that's on its
back, empty like
a burnt tobacco can.

It'll be another hour
to Missoula at this rate
and still I see idiots
trying to pass,
fishtailing into the snowy
berm.
...*Falling in love,*
it occurs to me,
is like driving in the snow.
Even with good tires
and decent skills
there's no guarantee
against bad breaks
and blind spots.

Indian Blankets

I set out watercolors and jars of water
as children arrive, their usual hubbub
a contrast to the lump in my throat.

Today is our long-awaited project for Native Stories:
paintings of loved ones at sunrise
kept warm by woven blankets.

But last night a 7th grader
hung himself, in apparent suicide
and my students don't yet know.

I wait, as instructed until after the pledge.
They stare.
Some tear up.

Others say, "That happened
to my Auntie,"
or "I've been to a lot of funerals."

They work quietly, diligently, producing rich
reds, oranges, greens,
Navajo blankets, Blackfeet, Salish,

a few Western-style, long braids in deep black.
Roger paints the sky red
around pencil-drawn stars;

Christian sketches a woman
alone, the wind
swirling her campfire smoke into the sky.

Halfway through class Nakota asks for a pass,
returns tear-stained, crumbles into my arms
his big 6th grade body shaking.

No one laughs or makes fun.
We hang the paintings in the hall;
a small act, this affirmation of life.

Compass

My father reads to me from a box of letters
over the phone:
In 1873, Alvira Wright McWhirk
traveled by wagon train from Ohio
to the Bitterroot Territory of Montana.

We are incredulous
and eager: this unknown envelope
of family history—the same path
I chose so randomly
a century past her death.

Other names trickle down:
Cora Henrietta
with a child's grave in Missoula,
Horace, and Henry
at St. Stephen's Episcopal Church.

For weeks, my brain is alive with
the cream walls of Ohio farm kitchens,
the churn of wooden wheels
the butterscotch scent
of ponderosa pines.

Did she live beside the Salish
as I do now?
Was the Bitterroot for her, too,
strange and familiar?
Is this why, upon arriving

I drove instinctively south—
to Stevensville, then north—to the Jocko
to dream, blindly,
behind red eyelids
at Arlee?

As if, casting
search lines
across the continent
she pressed
onward—

Red Moon Girl

Two authors visit for National Poetry month:
    Robert Lee (white beard, black beret, pearl earring)
    Jennifer Finley (Salish-Cree, bird tattoos, questions shaped like taffy)
and words pop from the least expected pencils.

Danny furrows his brow, so much misspelled, lines wobbly:
    Silence is the sound of the wind
        the smell of air
        the taste of pie in the evening.
    It is the touch of a soft cloth when rubbing your face.

Richard centers his neatly:
    Sitting, listening, watching for
        silver flash in
    the shallows.   *Eagle awaits—*

Eugene is so curious he comes down from 8th grade and hovers in the corner:
    I am from fry bread and riverbed stones
    Like the breeze I am calm and slow,
        in search of the unknown
    One spirit out of many

Just before we thank our guests, Linnea reads hers, quiet, firm:

    I am a girl from many tribes
    Blackfeet, Pend d'Oreilles and Kootenai

    I am born from a red moon with roses
    I am Red Moon Girl.

    I dance for a flower which hasn't bloomed
    I pray hard for that flower, my sister

    I see worth in the stars
    I make art with those stars

    My hands full of colors from paint
    that drips from the canvas
    I am Red Moon Girl.

When Falling, Dive

They climbed the trestle at Mission Dam,
the youth home boys,
bodies shivering
in the breeze
cropped heads of hair bent forward
to check out the water:
emerald green out aways
but murky and dark below the drop.
Only one way down
flying
from God knows what
but not thinking about that now—
Only the impending
slice of water and
freedom of limbs in its embrace

I watch beside my stalling Toyota
"Go Rupert! Woo-hoo, Bridger!
Yes, Elijah—
YES!"
And envy, if nothing else,
their courage
to surrender.

Bitterroot

In the spring
near the edges of snow
on gravelly, dry, soil
the bitterroot
opens
teardrop sepals, white, purple, pink
delicate and strong.

Spetlum, my Salish students call it,
and talk about the old woman
whose prayer brought it to being:
that despite desert drought,
brutal winters,
it would bear sustenance
for her children.

"Once," we read, from a field guide,
"seeds traveled with Meriwether Lewis,
pressed between the pages of his diary"
...Across the continent
and sprung to life—
unaffected by thirst,
Lewisia Rediviva.

The first week of May
is tender, giddy at school.
We teachers funnel the energy
with tempera
and construction paper
until a painted garden
sprouts

120 rectangles
floating down the hallway
petals, white roots—
the orange-colored "heart"
Always (the children tell me),
always placed back in the ground,
so it can grow.

Jessica Jones holds a Masters in English from the University of Montana, with licensure to teach grades 5-12 English and K-12 Art, as well as training in Indian Education for All (IEFA). She has taught on the Flathead Reservation and in Missoula and with students from the Blackfeet Reservation via University of Montana's Upward Bound.

Jones' poetry and essays have appeared in *Journal of the Assembly for Expanded Perspectives on Learning* (2014), the *Ohio Journal of Language Arts* (2014), *Poems Across the Big Sky II: An Anthology of Montana Poets* (Many Voices Press, 2016), *Bright Bones* (Open Country Press, 2018) and NCTE's *English Journal* (2018). She has also served as Writer in Residence for Calcutta Mercy Hospital in India, and with the Cuyahoga Valley National Park in Ohio. She is currently full-time faculty at Kent State University at Stark, where she teaches poetry, creative writing, and composition courses that focus on diversity and social justice.

She can be reached by email at jessicamariejones.mail@gmail.com and via her website at https://naea.digication.com/jessica_jones.

CPSIA information can be obtained
at www.ICGtesting.com
Printed in the USA
BVHW031128240319
543510BV00001BA/23/P

9 781635 348859